Simple

Thoughts

on Finding

Love and

Marriage

Please visit the Hay House
Website at: **www.hayhouse.com**

What Readers Are Saying about
*Simple Thoughts on Finding Love
and Marriage*

*"Your ability to express your thoughts
so beautifully is truly a gift from God.
Each time I read your book, I find
hidden beauty in your words."*— E.R.

"I use Simple Thoughts *as a medita-
tion book and as a gift to my clients
and other psychotherapists."*— T.G.

*"I have just ended a serious relation-
ship and find your words of wisdom
very comforting. We were not right for
each other, but I know that my perfect
love will be here soon."*— M.M.

Simple Thoughts on Finding Love and Marriage

Anne Meridien

Hay House, Inc.
Carlsbad, CA

Copyright © 1997 by Anne Meridien

Published and distributed in the United States by:
Hay House, Inc., P.O. Box 5100, Carlsbad, CA 92018-5100
(800) 654-5126 • (800) 650-5115 (fax)

Designed by: Christy Salinas

Library of Congress Cataloging-in-Publication Data

Meridien, Anne.
    Simple thoughts on finding love and marriage / Anne Meridien.
       p.   cm.
    ISBN 1-56170-428-8 (pbk.)
    1. Love. 2. Marriage.   I. Title.
BD436.M44   1997
306.81—dc21
                                   97-26203
                                   CIP

ISBN 1-56170-428-8

00 99 98 97   4 3 2 1
First Printing, December 1997

Printed in the United States of America

Preface

For the past six years, I have kept a personal journal. I write every single morning on plain white paper, yellow pads, or in composition books.

One day, I bought a beautiful malachite green and gold book, with gilt-edged blank pages and an elegant ribbon page marker. I placed it prominently on my bedroom dresser, deeming it far too pretty to write in.

Something sparked me to finally write in this treasured little book. I wrote intimate thoughts to myself, one line at a time, over a period of almost two years. I never intended for anyone else to read my personal affirmations on finding love.

One evening I decided to read my bedside journal. My experiences and feelings over several years were captured in slightly more than a few dozen phrases, like snapshots in a photo album. Valentine's Day was approaching. and I decided to make copies for a few close friends as a small gift.

I received heartwarming phone messages followed by thank-you notes. I was surprised

to hear or read, "I really love this," "I read it over and over," and "I keep it by the side of my bed." My single, 30-year-old friend liked it as much as my twice-divorced, once-widowed, 65-year-old friend. Both men and women called, asking for additional copies.

After much encouragement, I self-published my diary as a small gift booklet. I received wonderful mail from across the United States and abroad. A lovely letter from a man in England prompted me to seek a publisher who could distribute my book to a wider audience.

It is with tremendous gratitude that I thank Louise L. Hay for encouraging and supporting me in so many ways. When my book was selected for publication and distribution by Hay House, Inc., I knew that I was blessed. My sentiments are personal, but perhaps more universal than I realized. I'm thrilled to share my thoughts of life, love, and commitment with you and those you love, or hope to love.

— *Anne Meridien*

You deserve to

be loved

cherished, and

respected by a

person with

character who

is committed

to you.

You will
find love,
comfort, and
companionship.

Your emotional and physical health must come first.

Self-love and

self-care

precede

romantic and

faithful love.

Stay clear of
people who
gossip and lie,
who blame and
criticize, who
control through
silence, and
who are in too
much of their
own pain.

Take bold steps

to keep negative

people out of

your life.

Love will not

come until you

release all of the

pain and hurt

that is buried

deep inside

of you.

Overcome the
disappointments
of your past so
that you can
have the future
that you
deserve.

Let go of the
need to love
those who
cannot return
your love.
Detach from
the attachment.

Solitude is often required to heal the wounds of lost love, wrong love, unfaithful love, or toxic love.

Forgiveness
and solitude
will develop
your inner
strength and
immunity
from pain.

Embrace your

loneliness.

Be patient,

for love will

come again.

Replace
negative thoughts
and feelings with
images of beauty.
Cleanse your
heart, mind, body,
and soul.

Shadows may

pass over you,

but you must

never stand in

the darkness.

Sometimes the

darkness of

pain brushes up

against you to

jolt you into the

light of

God's love.

*Only by passing
through the
darkness can
you return to
the light of your
own soul.*

The sun shines.
The sun is
eclipsed by the
moon. You are
the sunlight of
your own life,
and others can
only cast
shadows for
short periods
of time.

Raindrops

cleanse the

earth and

punctuate life

with a melody

of freshness, by

night and day.

*Your teardrops
will kiss your
soul, washing
away debris
and setting you
free in the
sunshine of
your own life to
glisten and to
be happy.*

*With the
warmth of love
in your heart,
you will bask in
the light of
every moment,
every day
forever and
ever, and ever
and always.*

Develop

serenity and

security within

yourself.

Open a space in
your heart for
someone new.

You deserve someone special, so be your best self, today and every day.

Give love to

others for your

pleasure.

Recognize the

love others have

to share.

Receive others'

love in

whatever form

it takes.

Forgive
yourself for
the times you
were not loving.

Accept and

appreciate

yourself.

You are ready

to love again.

Be selective.

Be careful.

Accept nothing

less than the

best for

yourself.

Never settle for

just someone.

You will experience the complete fulfillment of love between a man and a woman.

You will celebrate the sensuality of love and friendship.

Love will come

when you are

happy.

You are

completely

ready now for a

bright, loving

person to walk

right into

your life.

You can attract a loving partner.

And so now it
begins — a new
life of love with
a kind and
gentle person
who cherishes
life as much as
you do.

Love is the freedom of spirit. No confinement. No criticism. No coercion. No guilt.

Your life was

meant to be

shared.

You will find

your partner.

You deserve

to be happily

married.

Only in the

form of

marriage can

you truly grow

in love with

another.

A marriage is coming, and you will fly like a bird in the sky, above the dark clouds.

Your partner
will be spiritual,
intelligent,
caring, and
faithful,
funny and dear
to your heart.

You will love

him or her as

he or she

loves you.

*Love is the
comfort in the
space between
two people.*

Love is trust

when there is

distance

between two

people.

Love is opening

your heart to

the feelings of

one another.

Love is

accepting your

past and

embracing your

future.

Love is
arriving in the
safe harbor of
commitment and
marriage.

Love is patience, hope, understanding, compassion, and unrelenting Faith.

Keep your life
simple and fill it
with love.

About the Author

Anne Meridien lives in Southern California with her son and daughter. She received her master's degree in speech pathology from San Diego State University. Anne is currently working in the areas of public relations and career development. She is an amateur photographer and enjoys the ongoing study of Feng Shui. She continues to keep a daily journal and is working on her second book.